Manga Drawing Lessons: Faces And Expressions

Pretty, Ugly, Cute: How to Draw Different Manga Faces

How to Draw Manga Faces

By: Gala Publication

2

Published By:

Gala Publication
ISBN-13: **978-1522802419**
ISBN-10: **152280241X**

©Copyright 2015 – Gala Publication

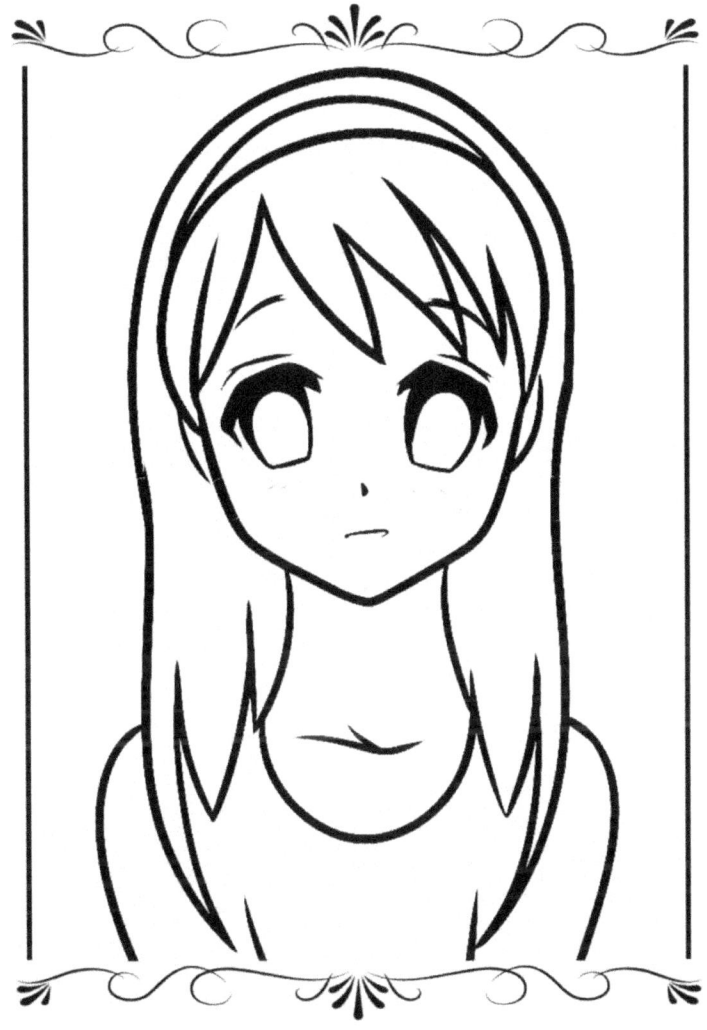

FACE 1

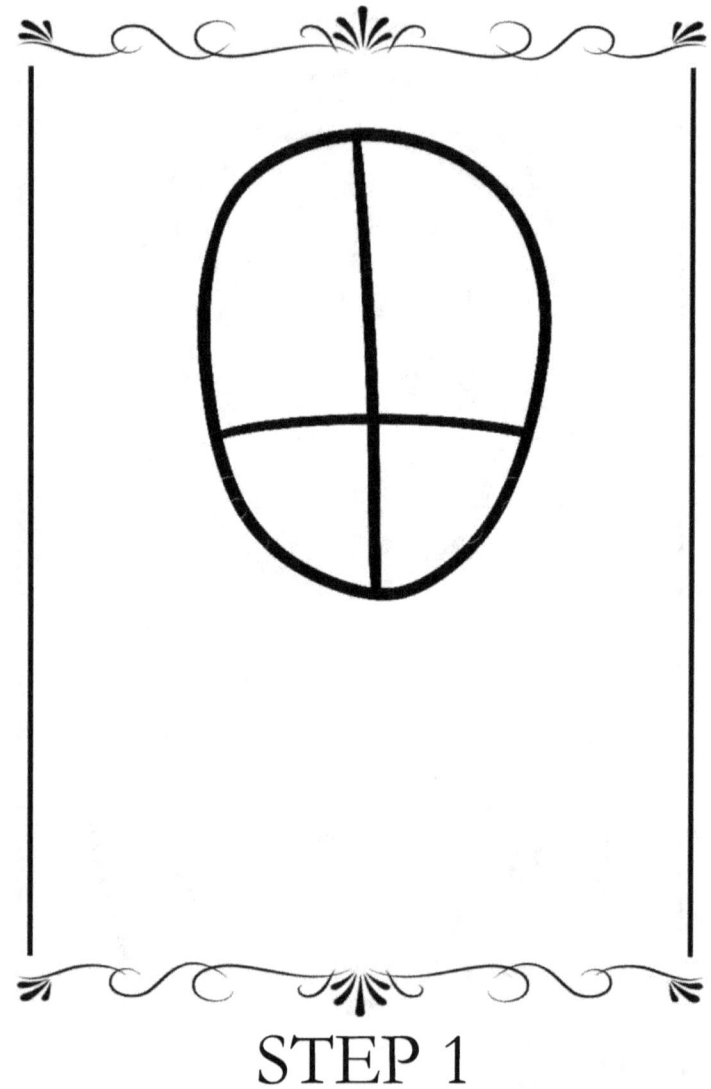

STEP 1

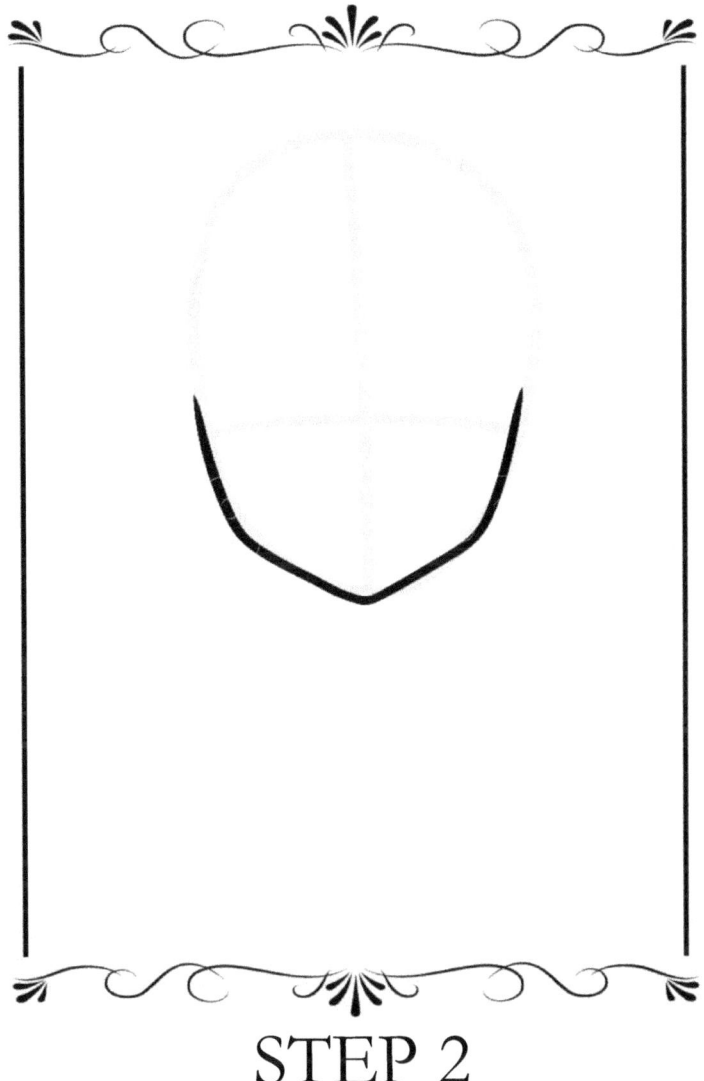

STEP 2

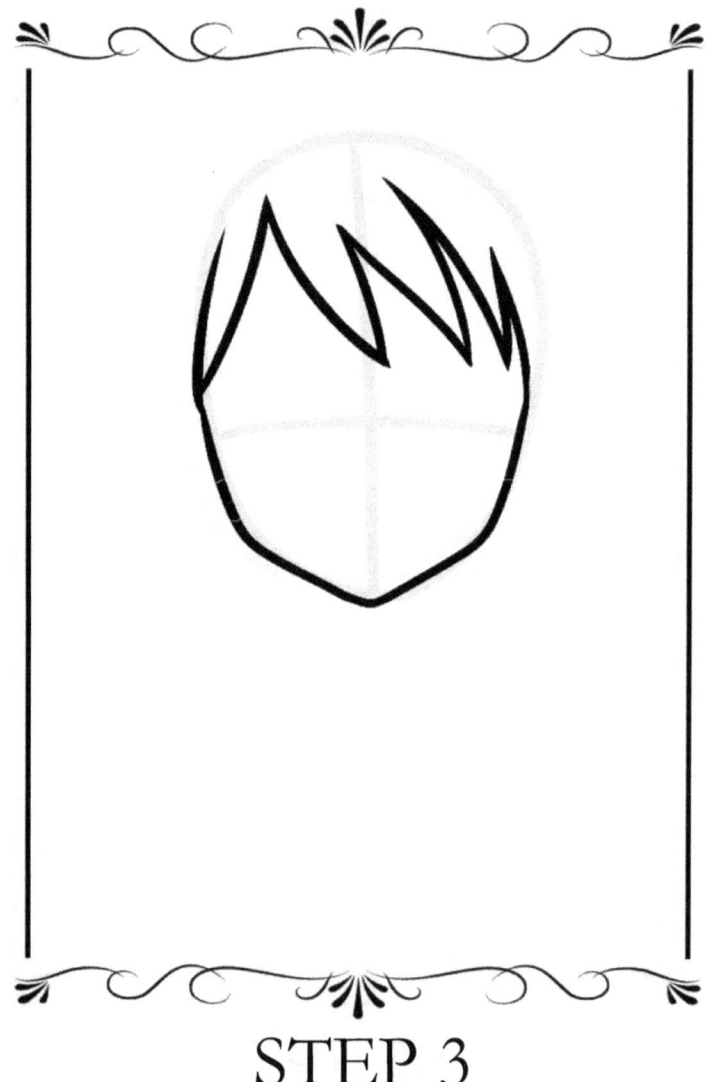

STEP 3

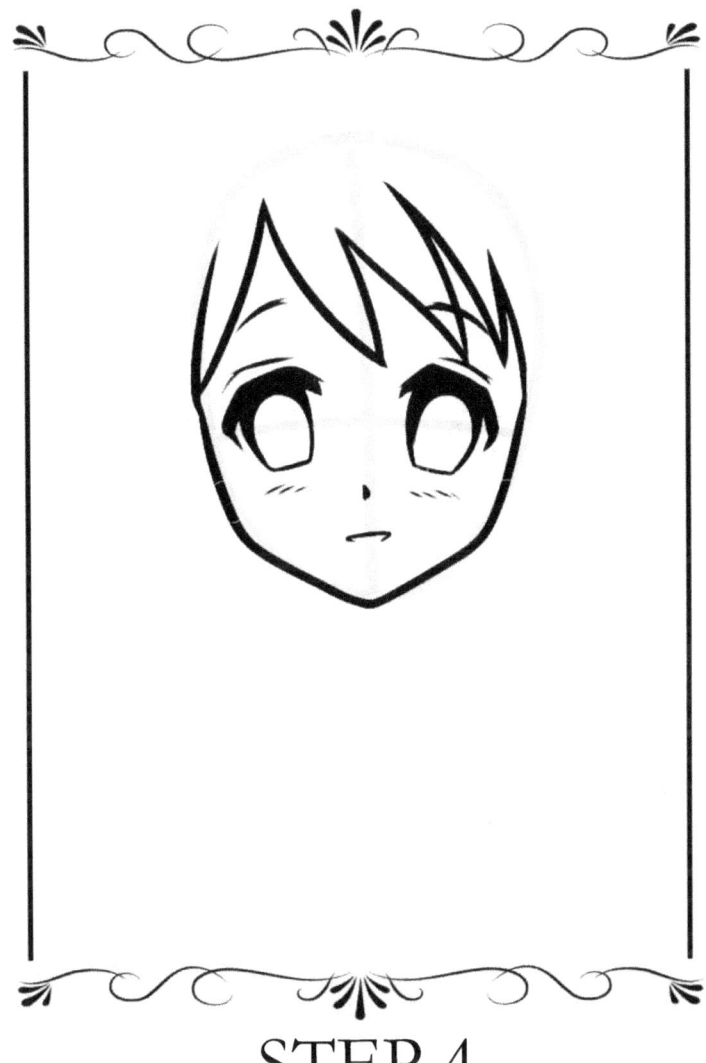

STEP 4

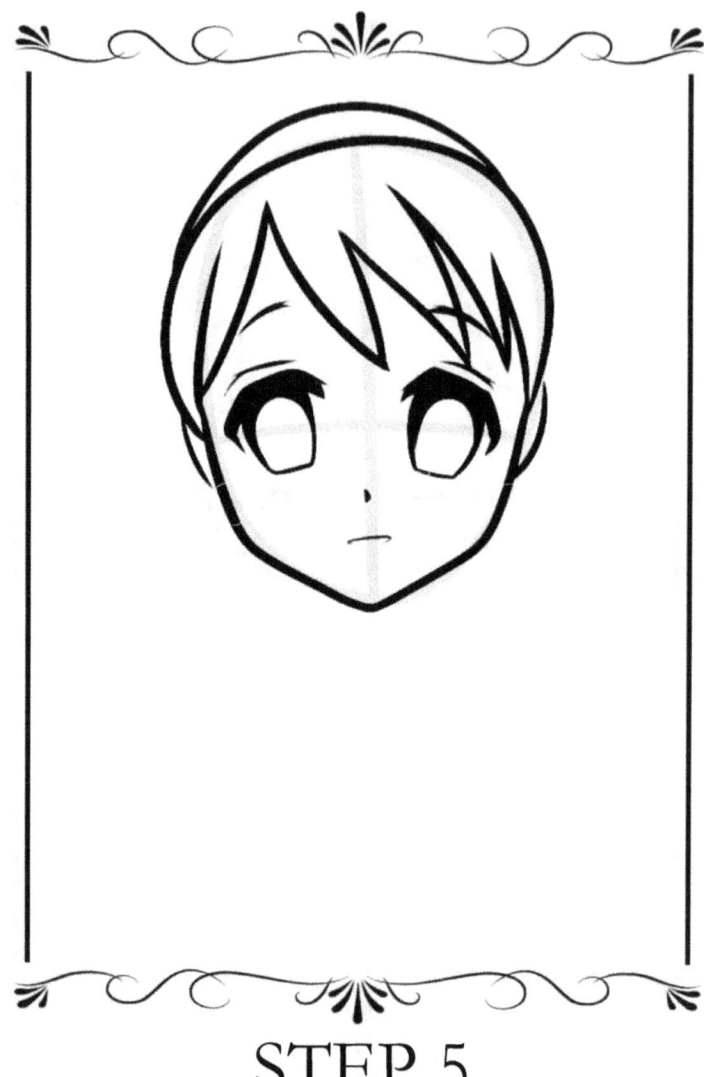

STEP 5

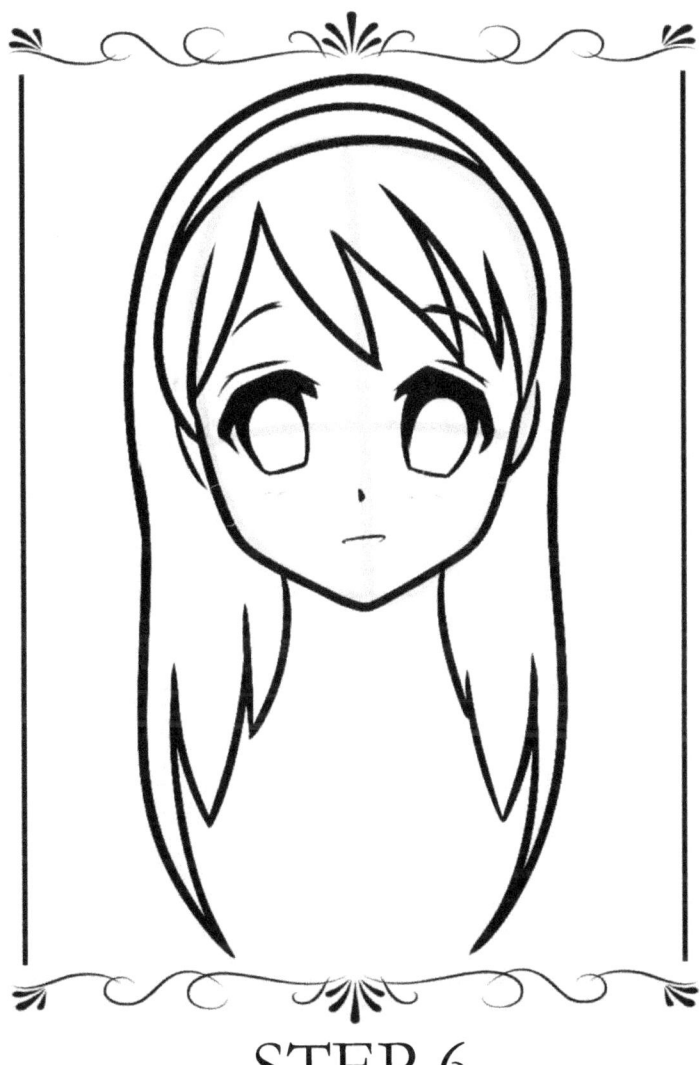

STEP 6

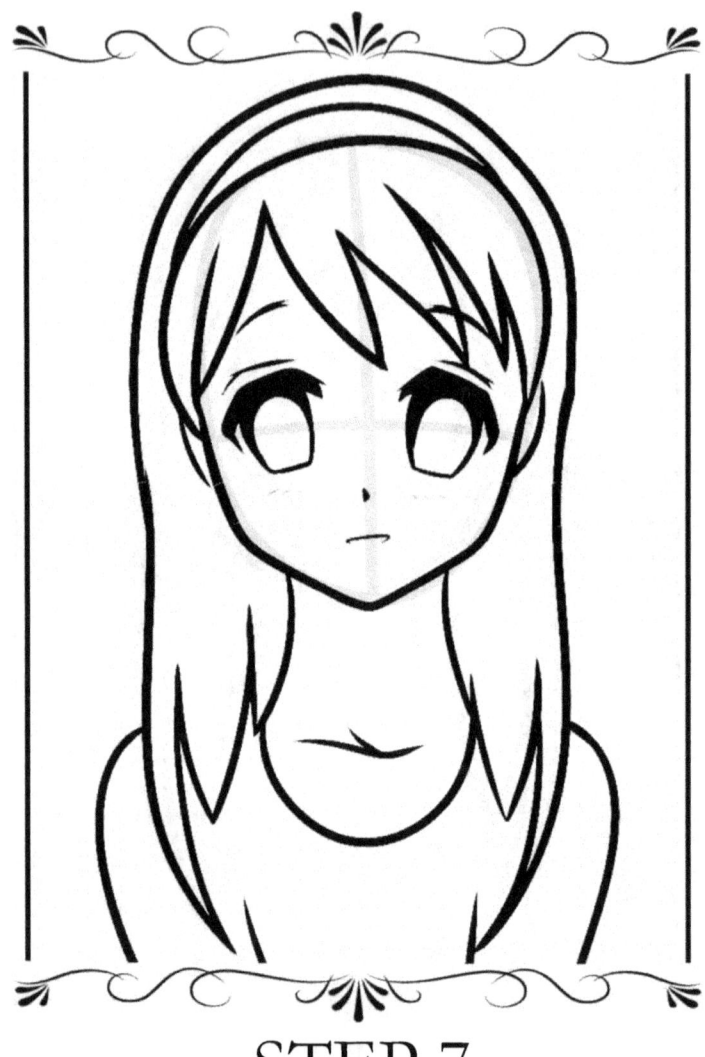

STEP 7

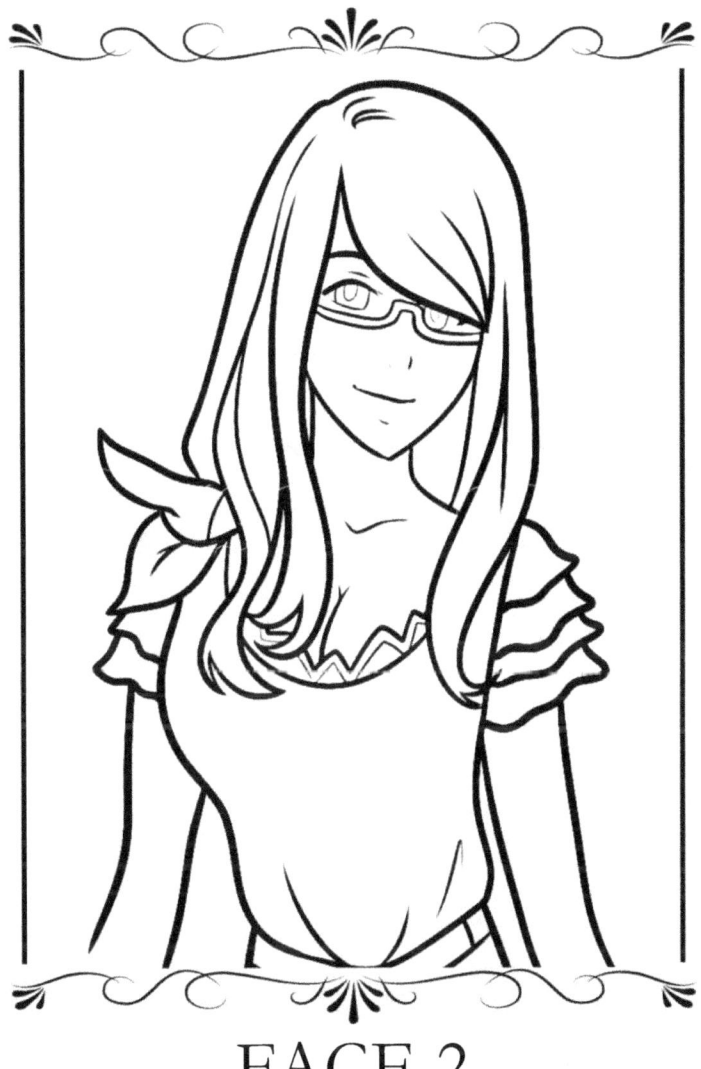

FACE 2

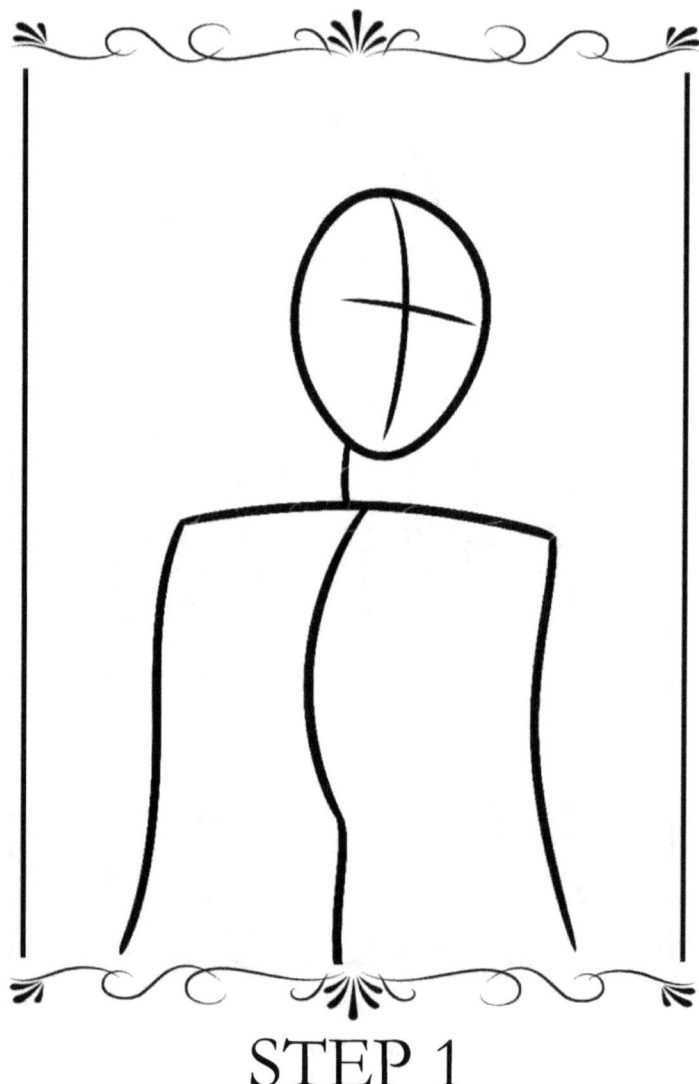

STEP 1

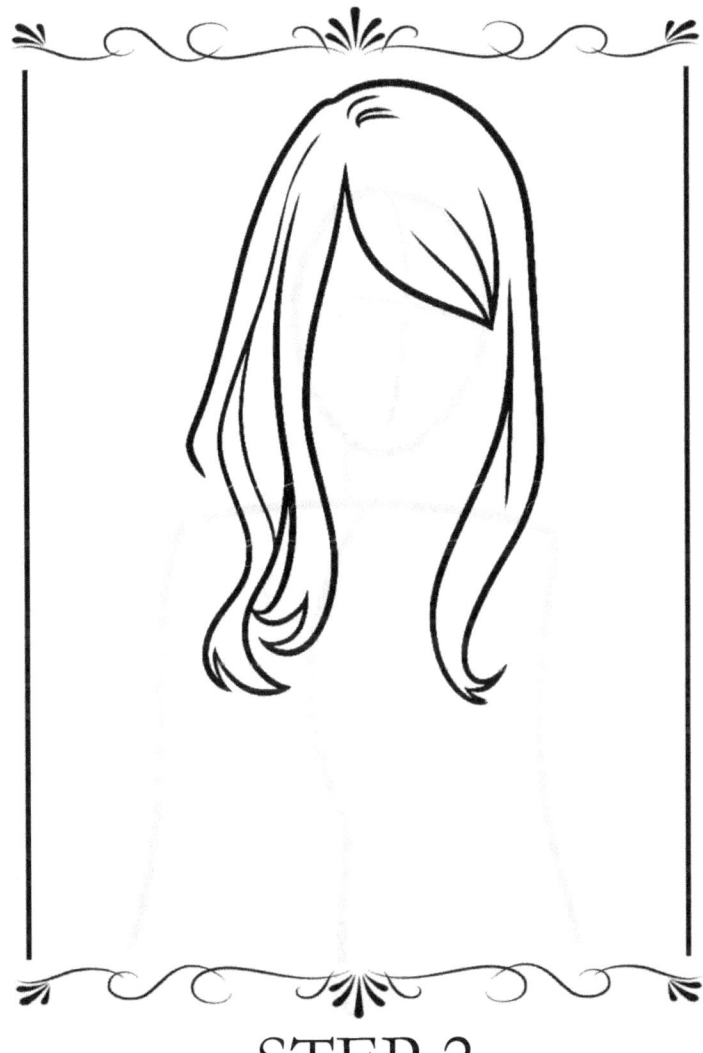

STEP 2

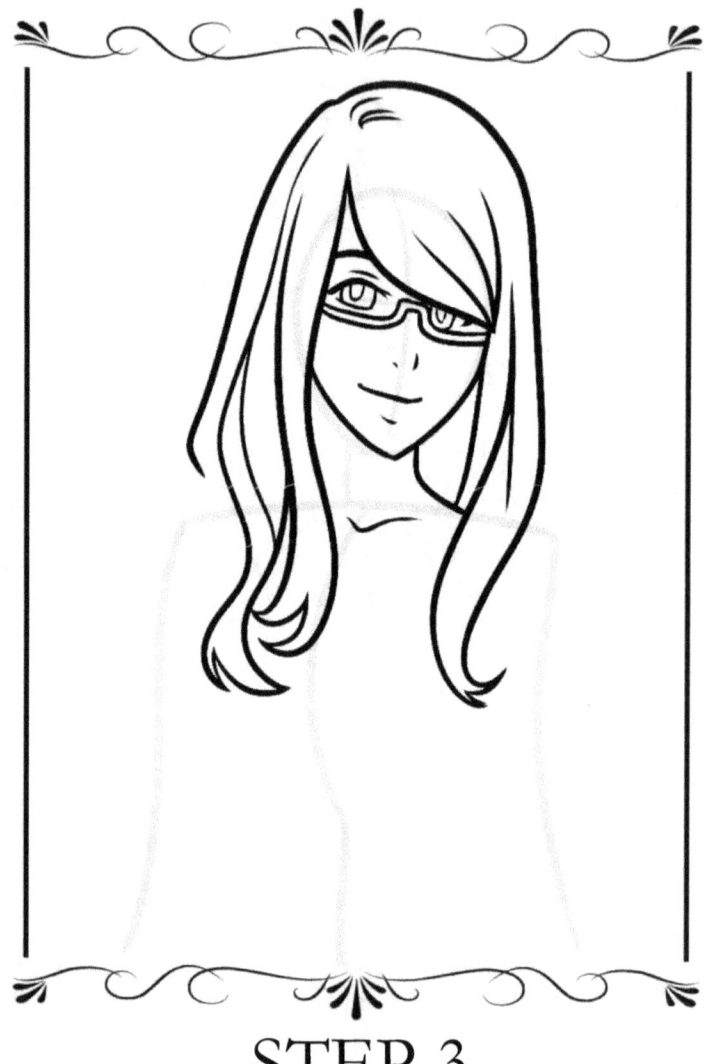

STEP 3

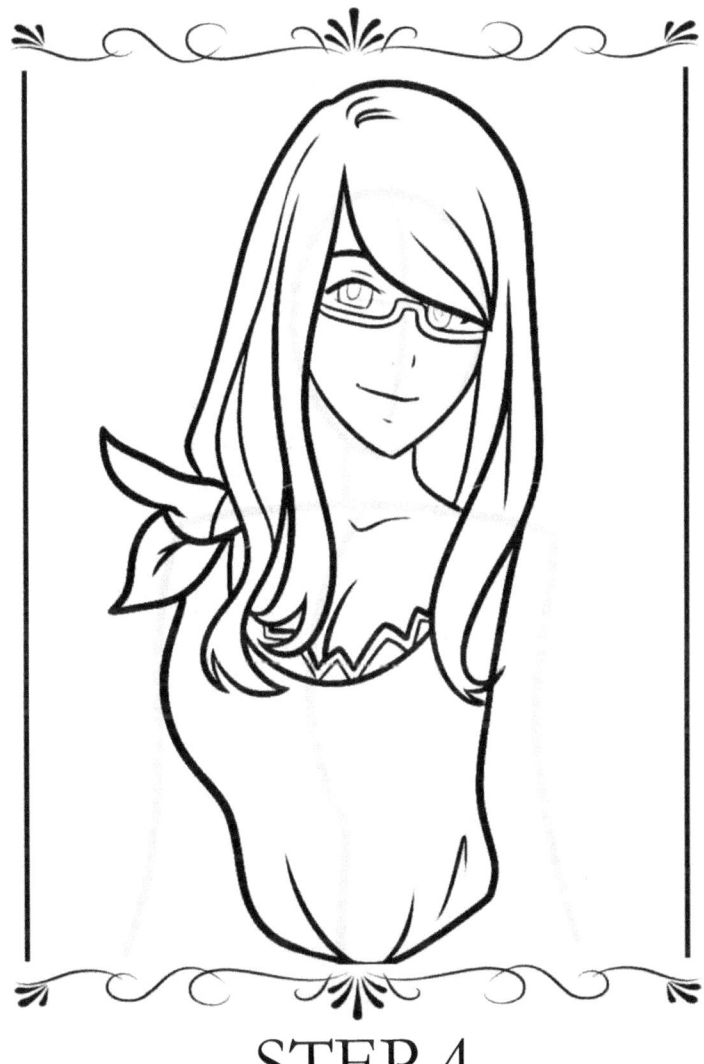

STEP 4

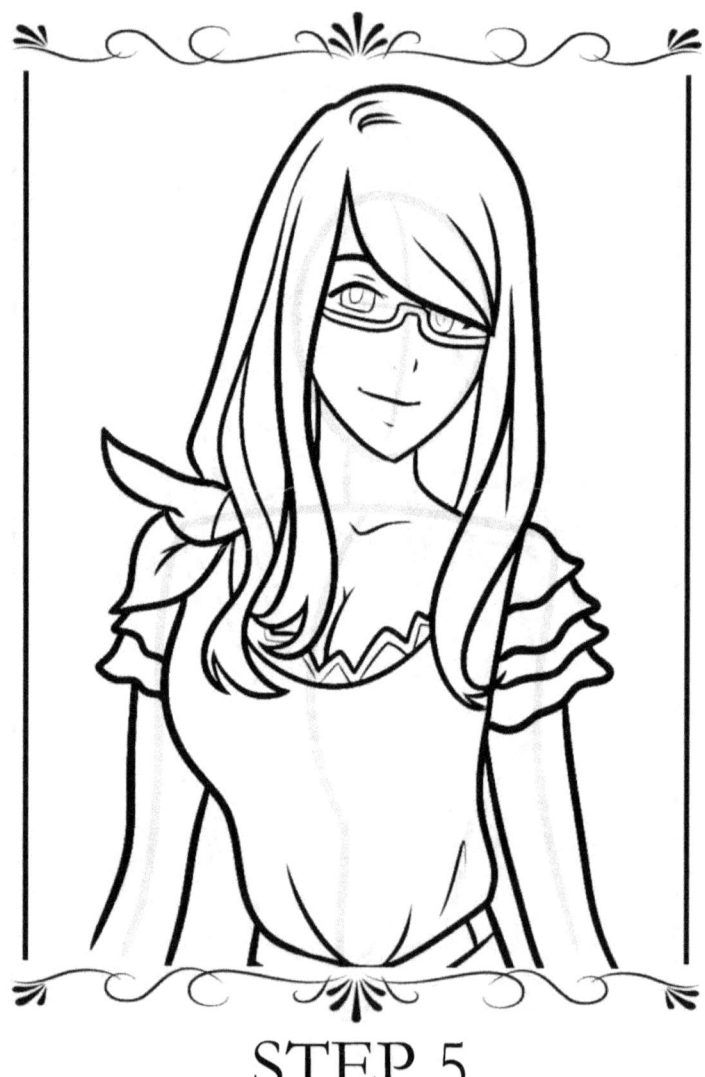

STEP 5

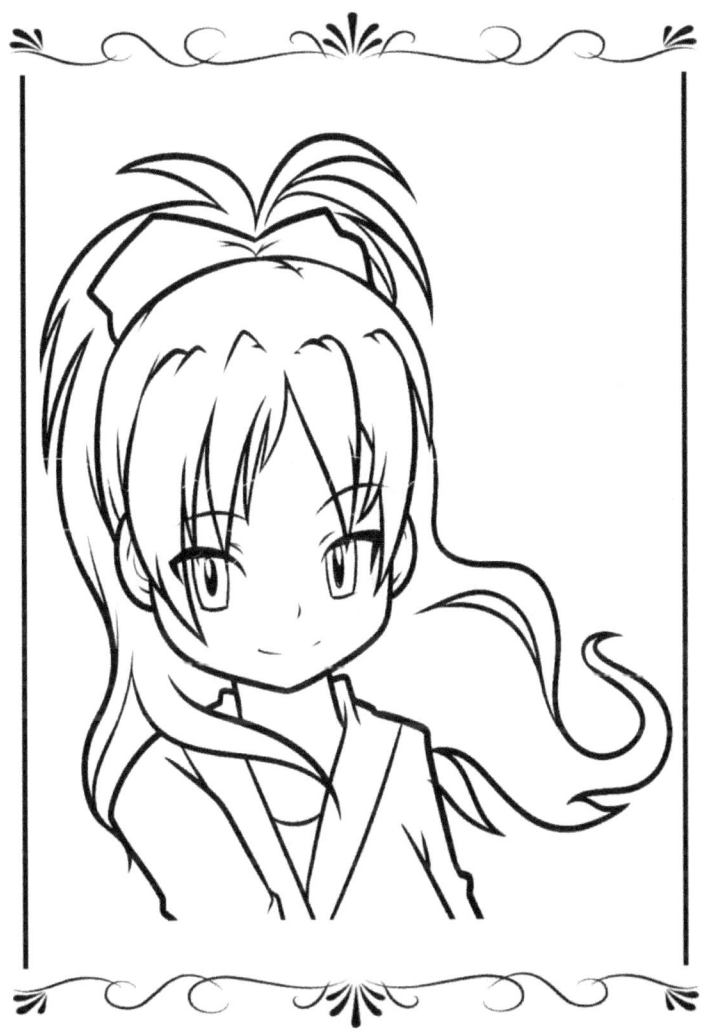

FACE 3

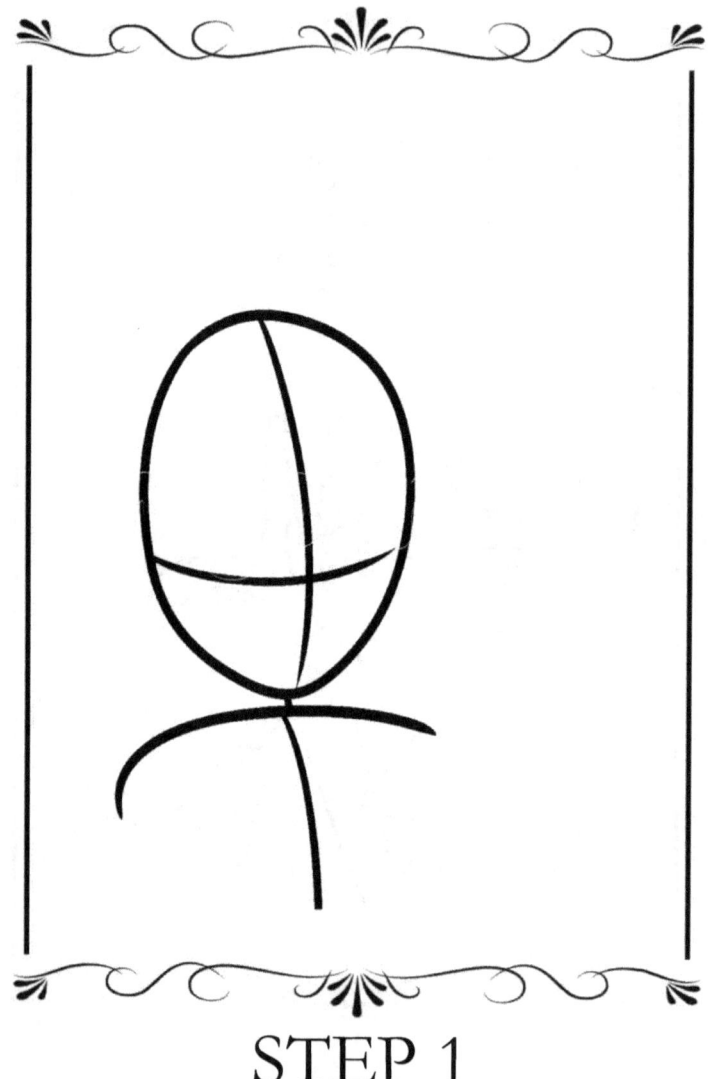

STEP 1

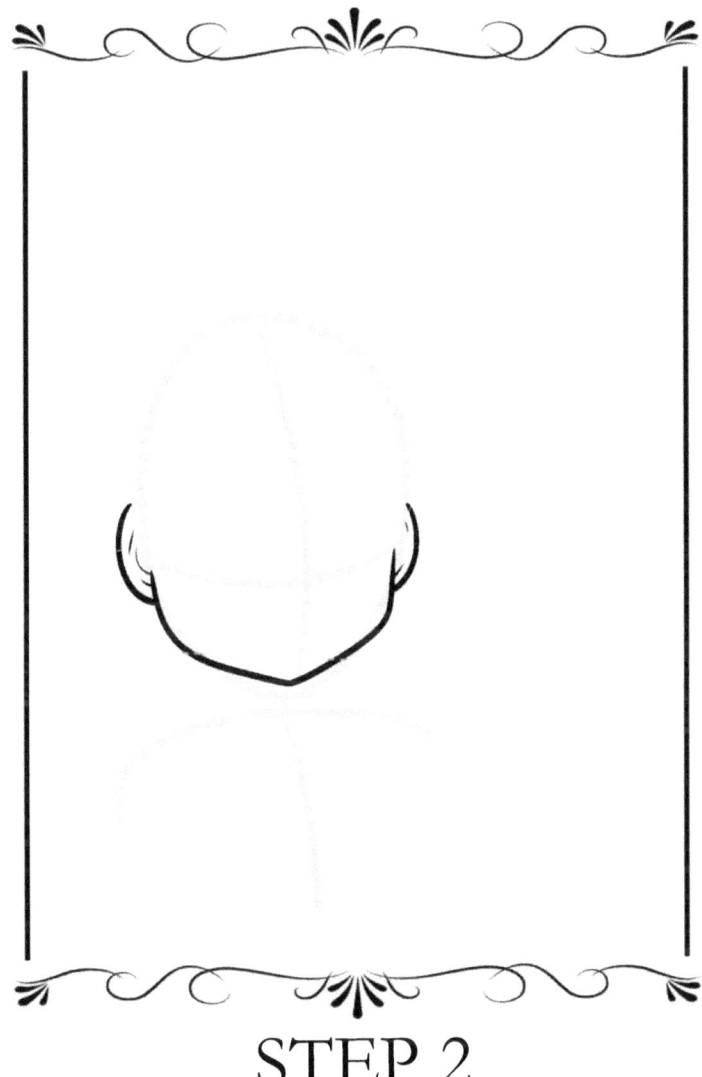

STEP 2

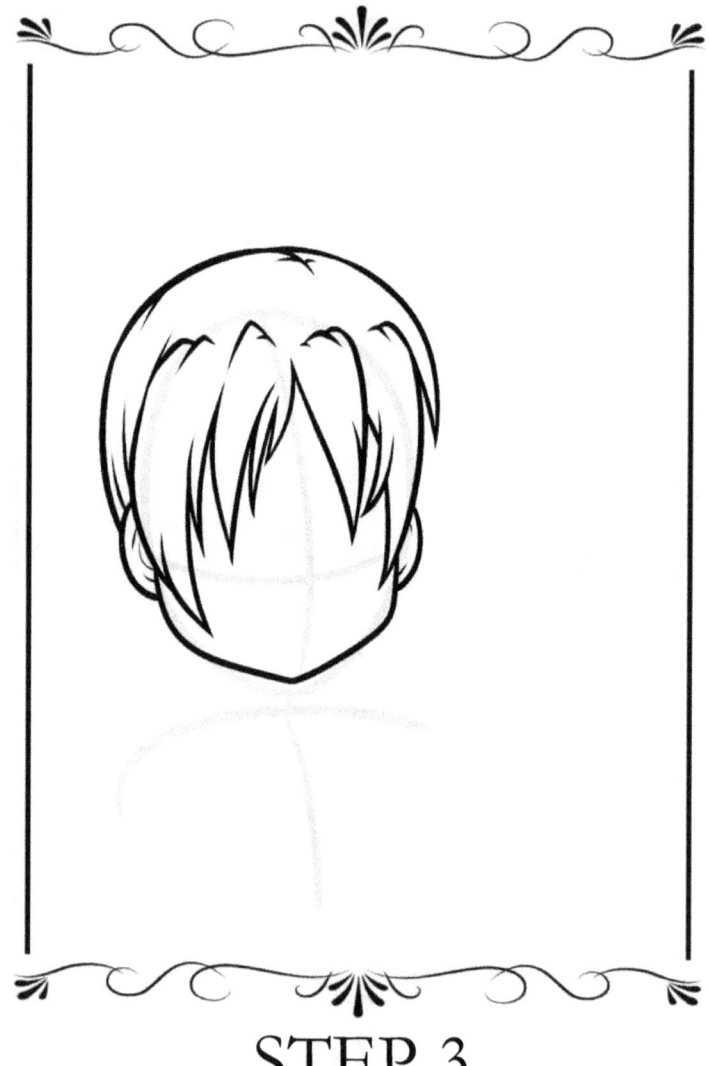

STEP 3

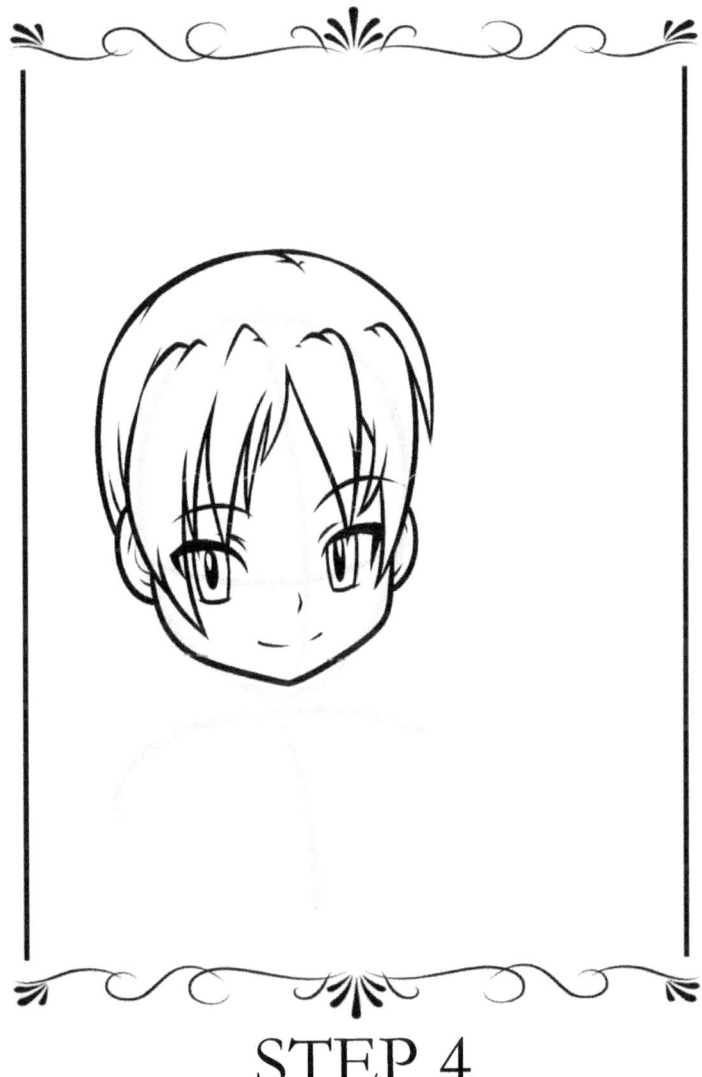

STEP 4

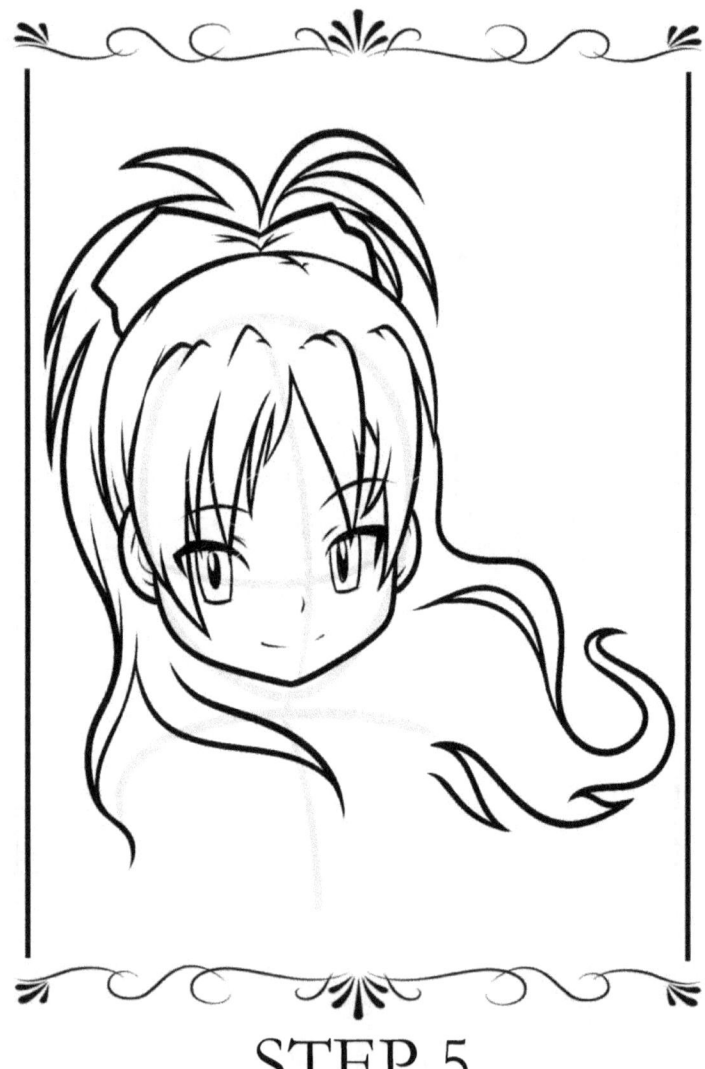

STEP 5

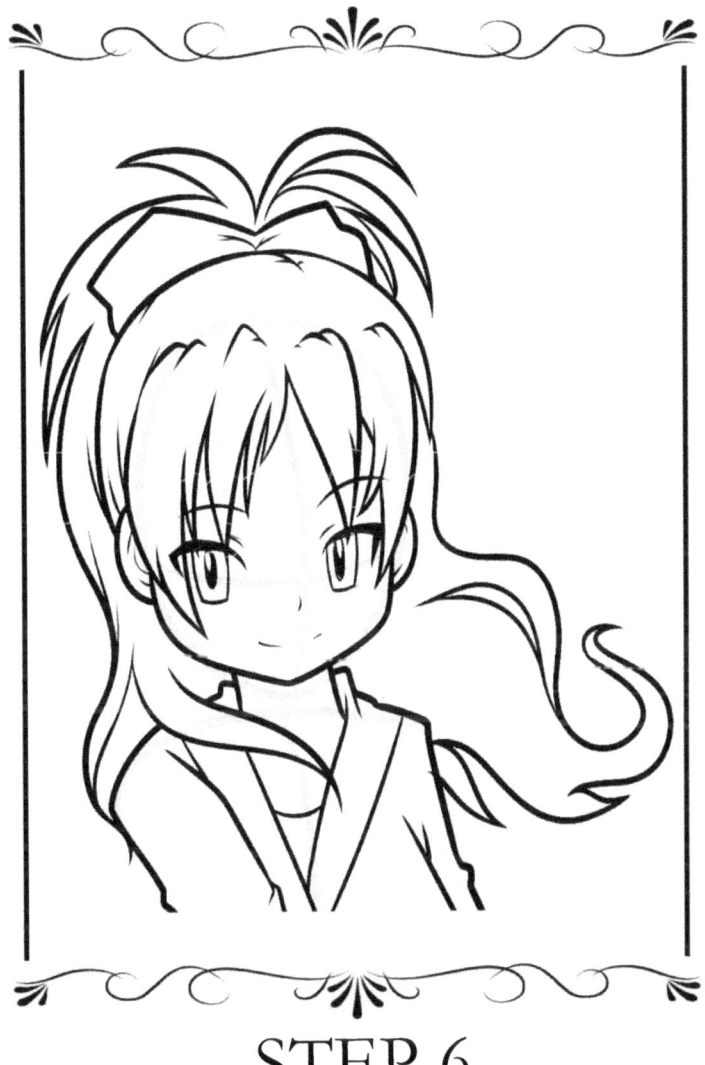

STEP 6

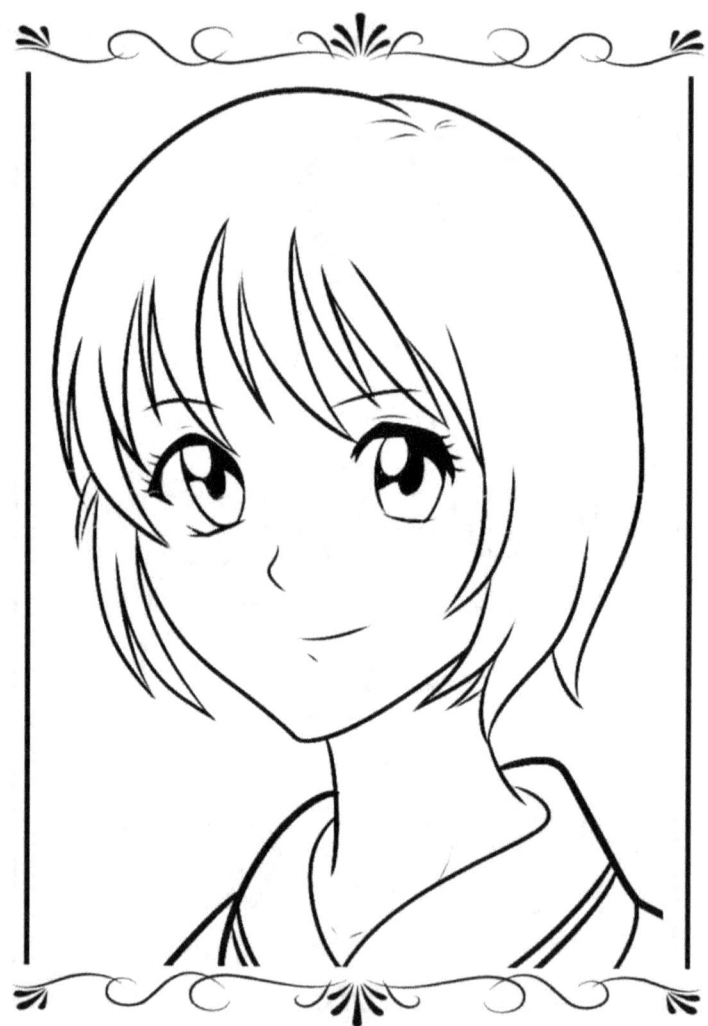

FACE 4

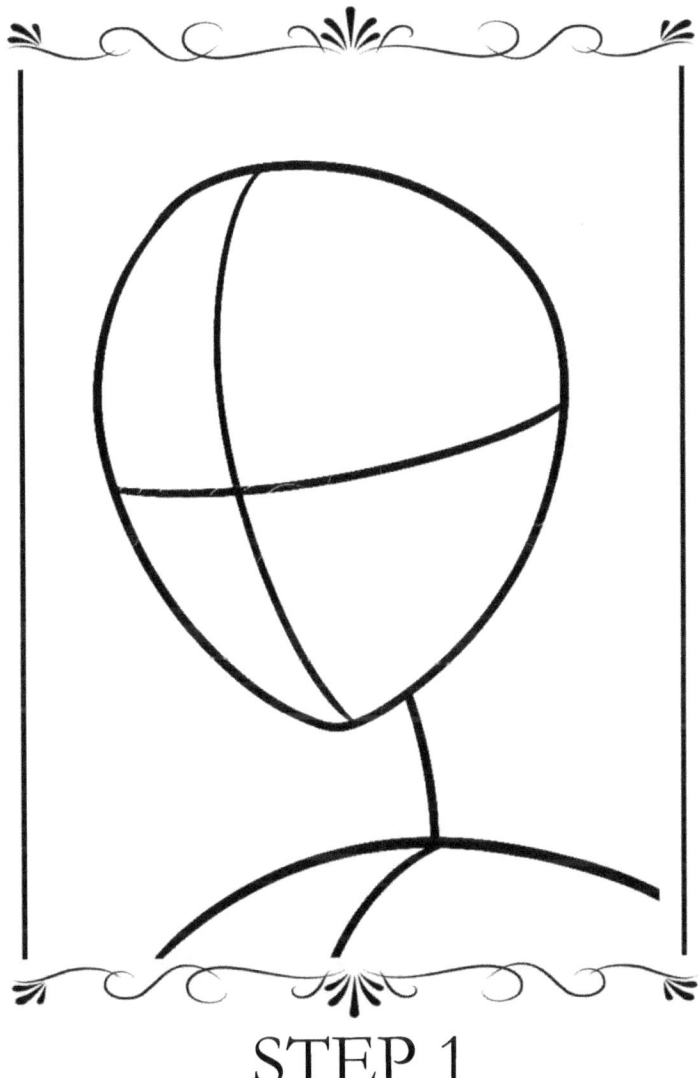

STEP 1

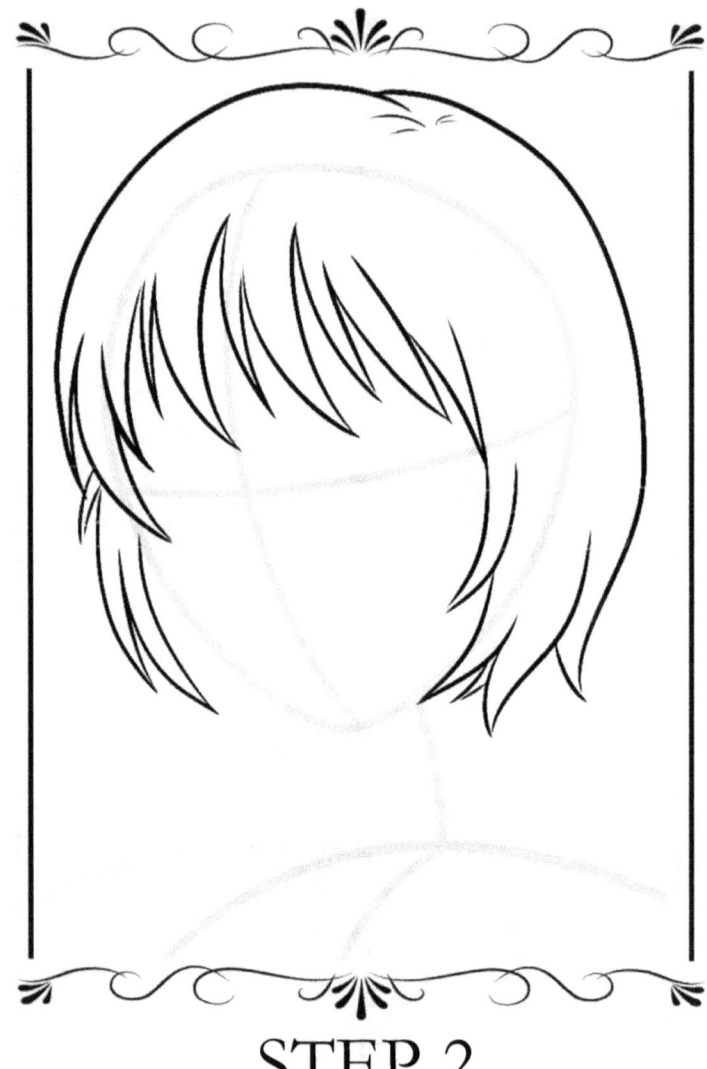

STEP 2

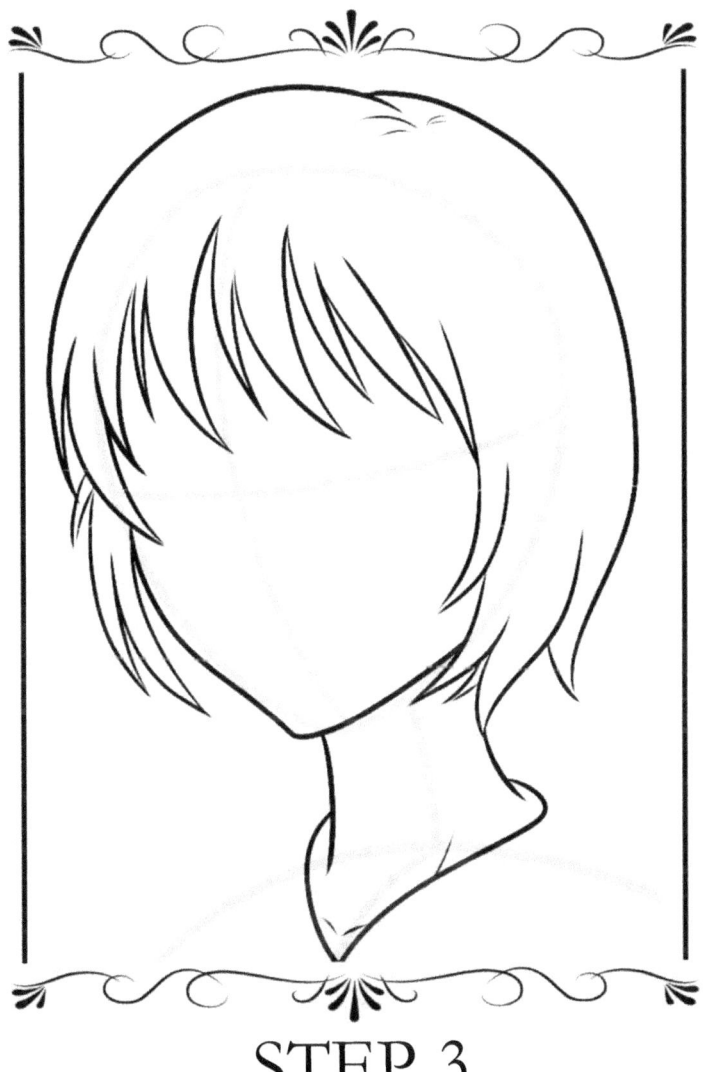

STEP 3

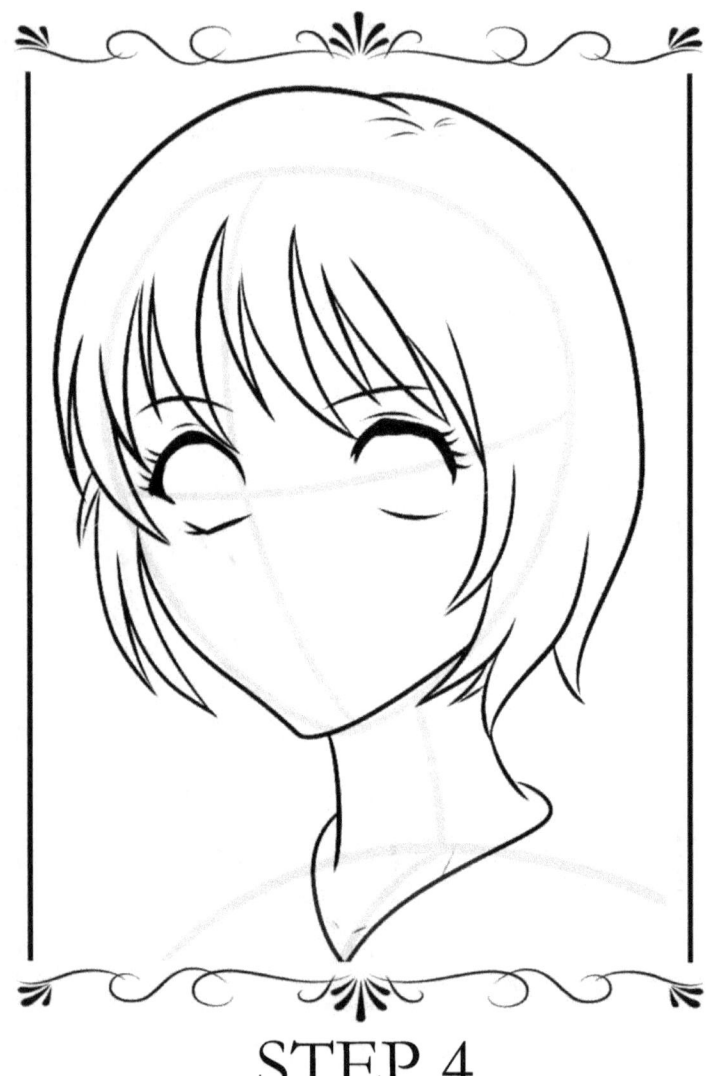

STEP 4

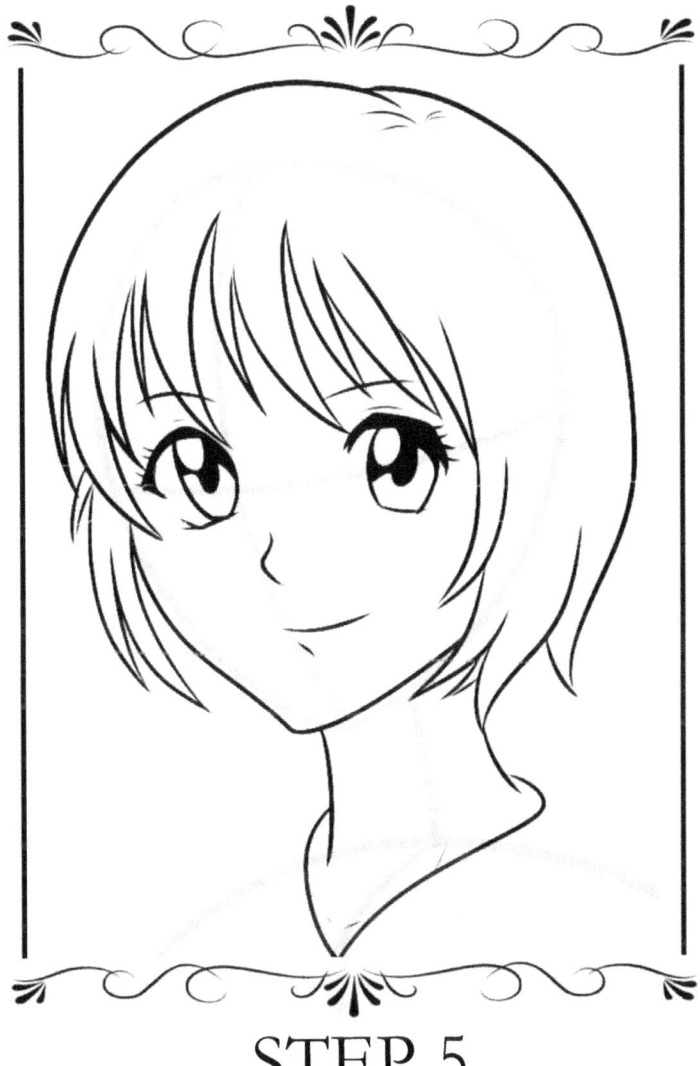

STEP 5

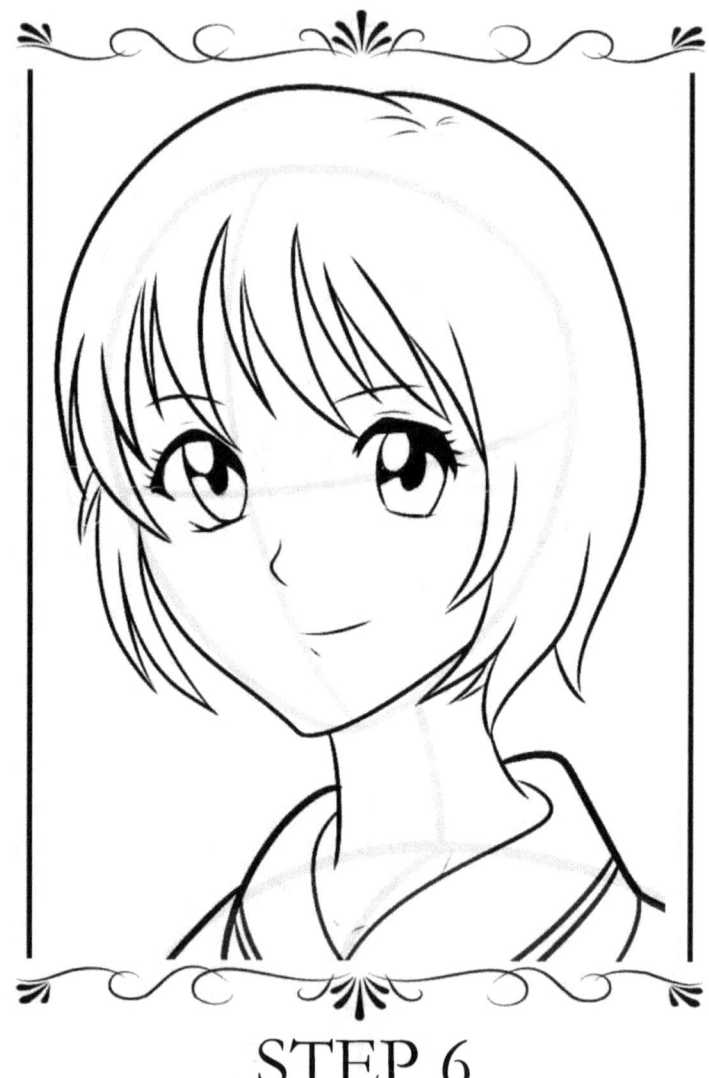

STEP 6

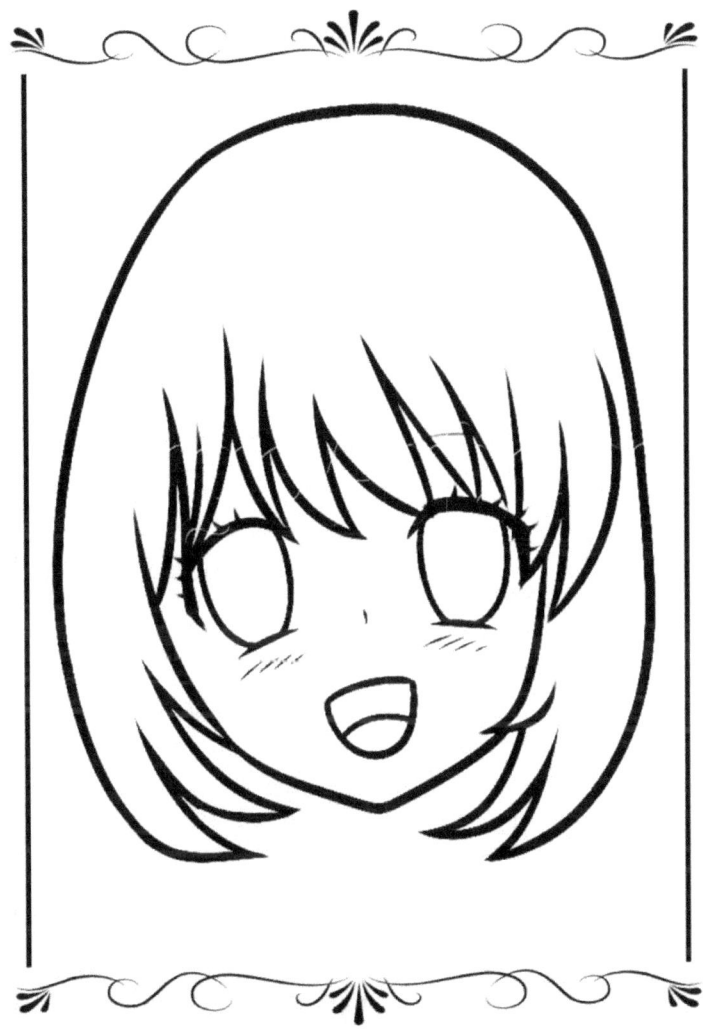

FACE 5

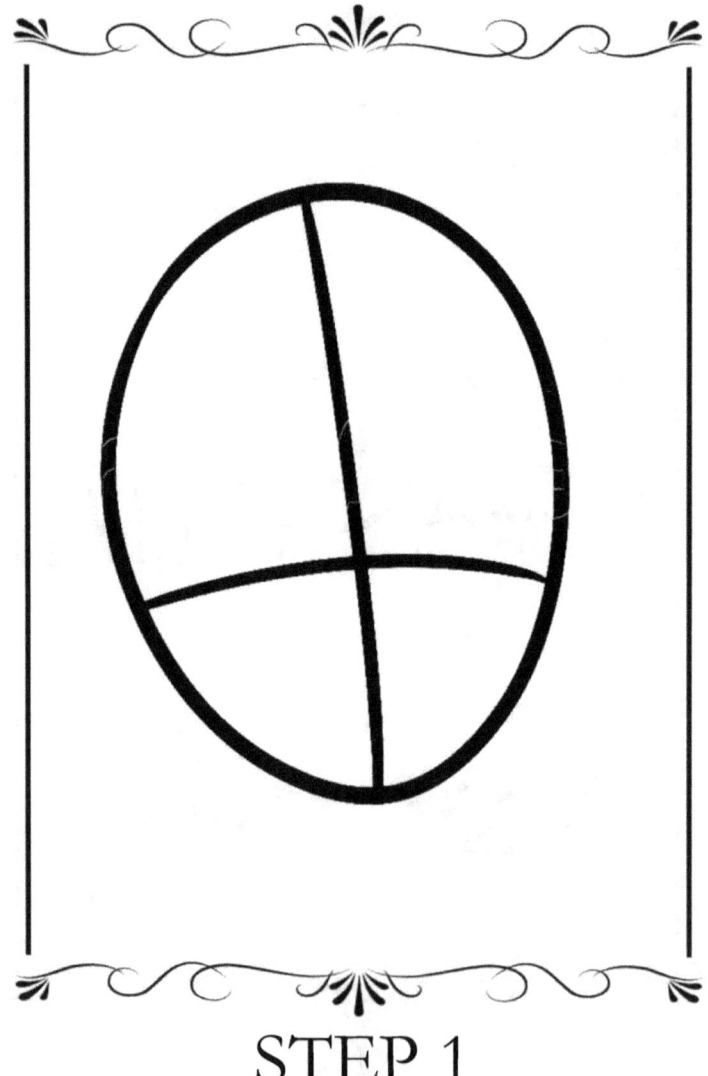

STEP 1

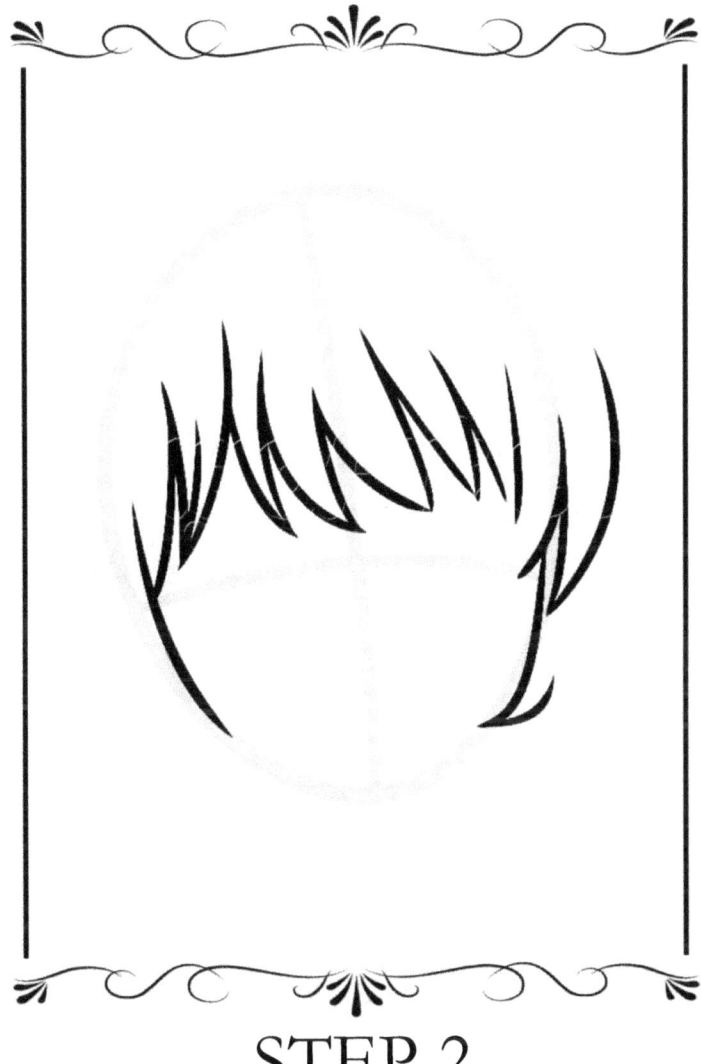

STEP 2

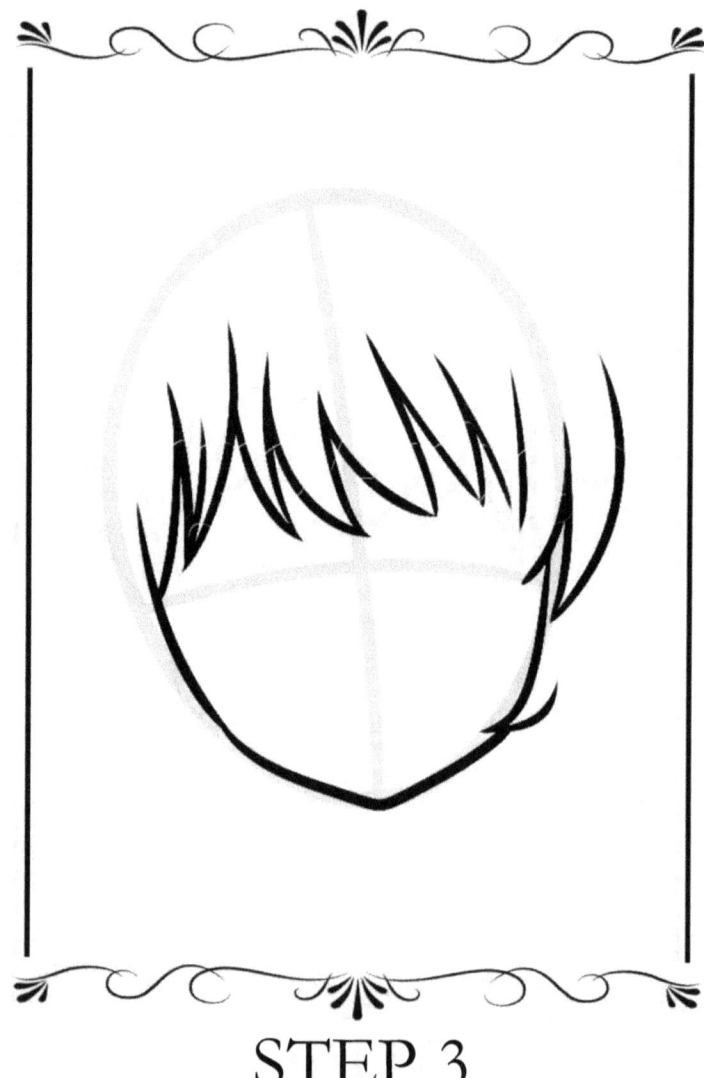

STEP 3

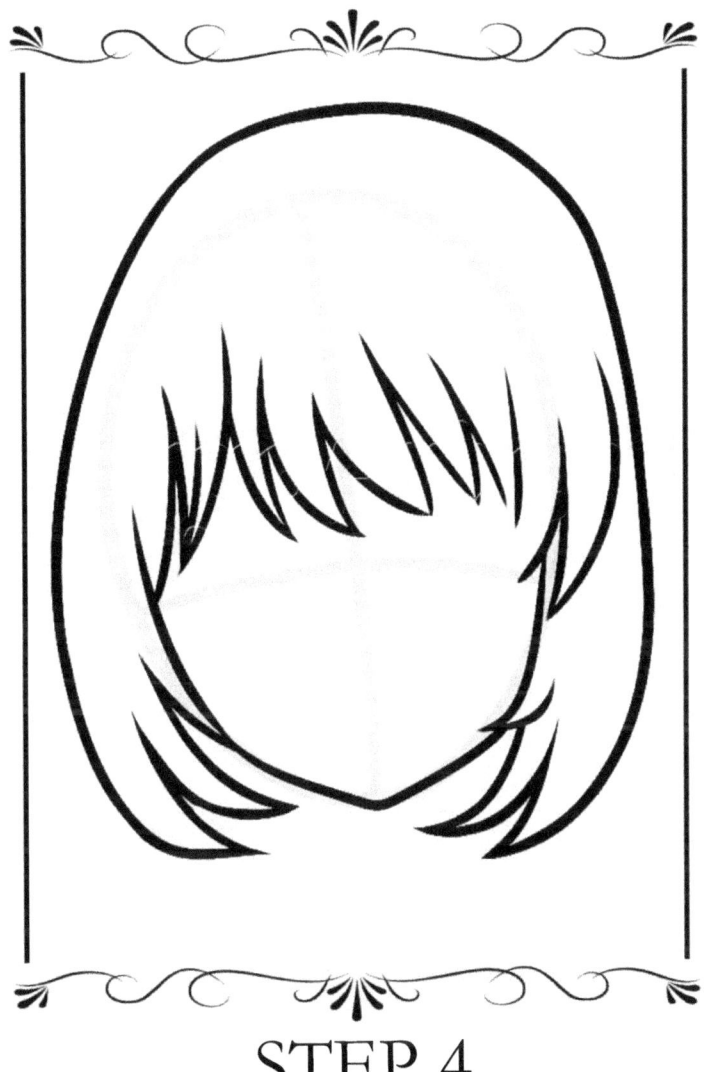

STEP 4

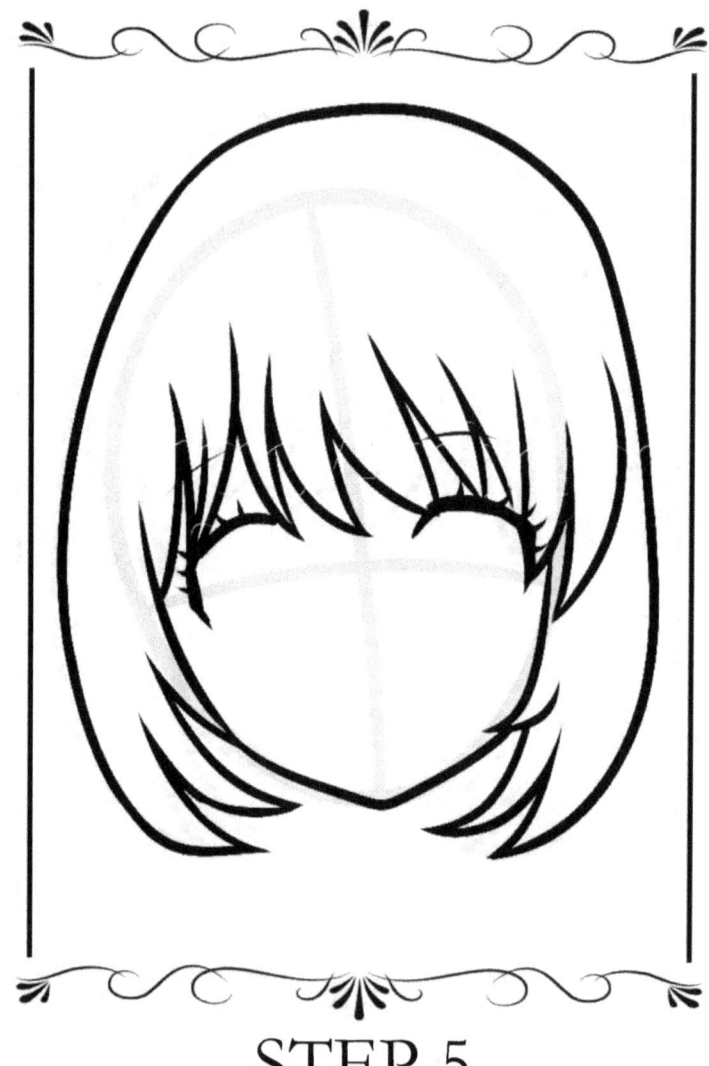

STEP 5

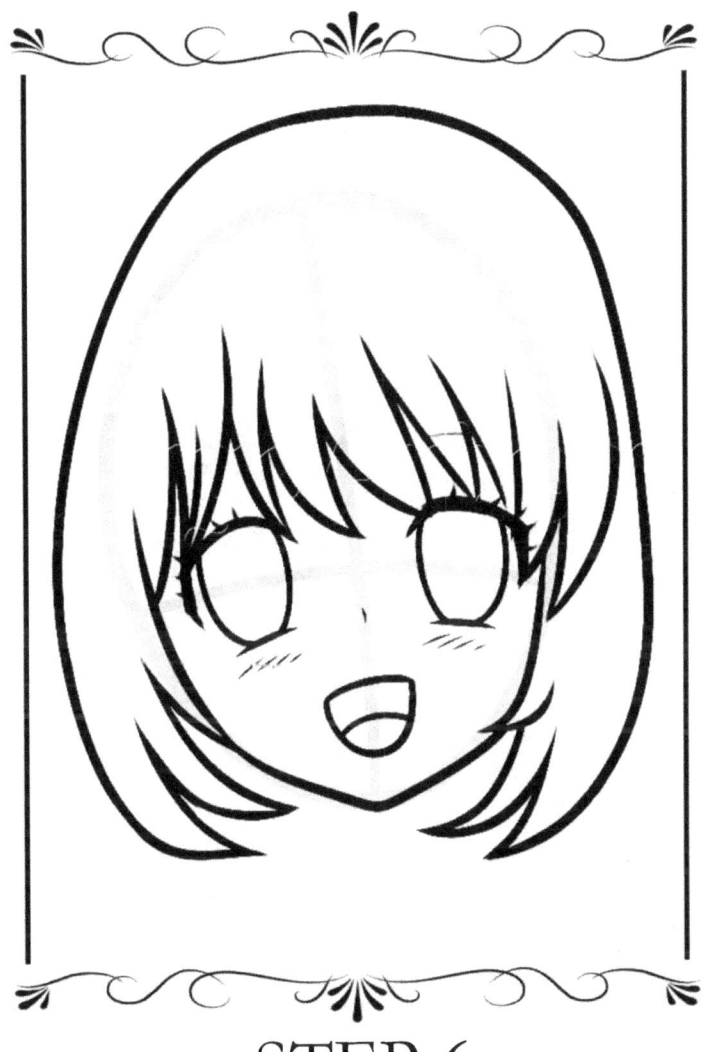

STEP 6

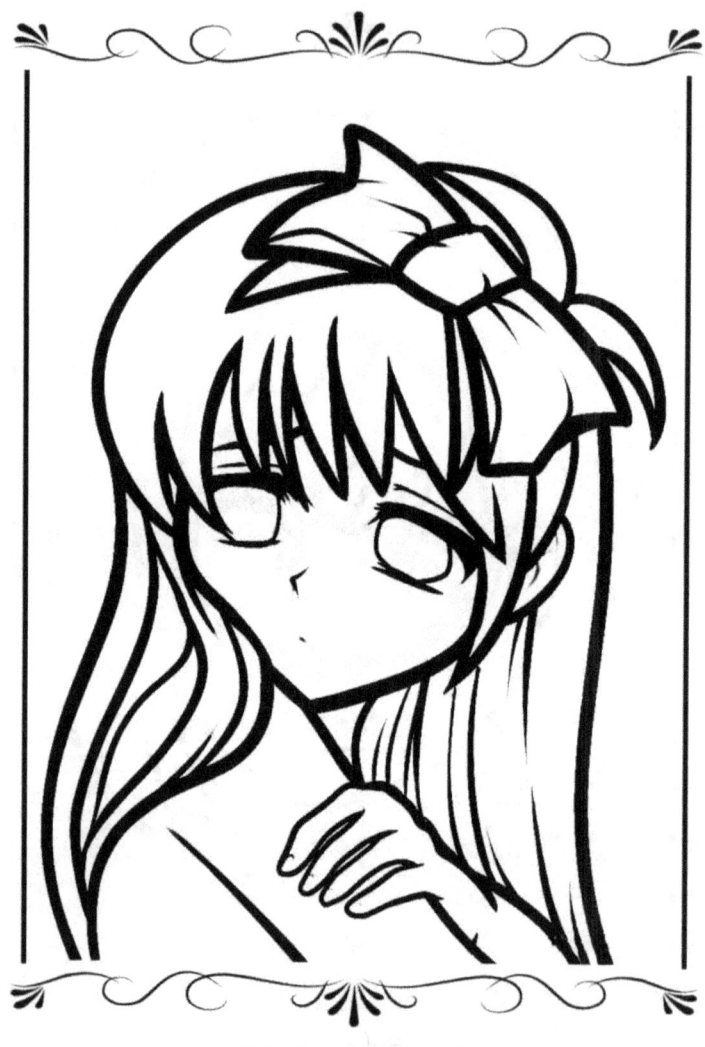

FACE 6

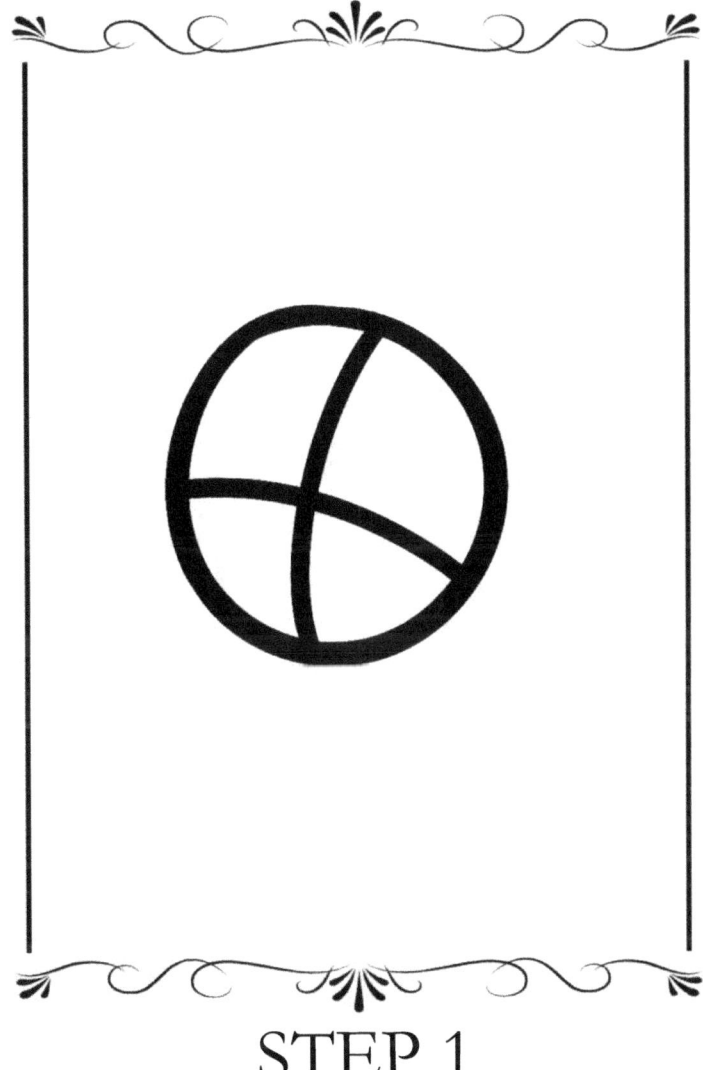

STEP 1

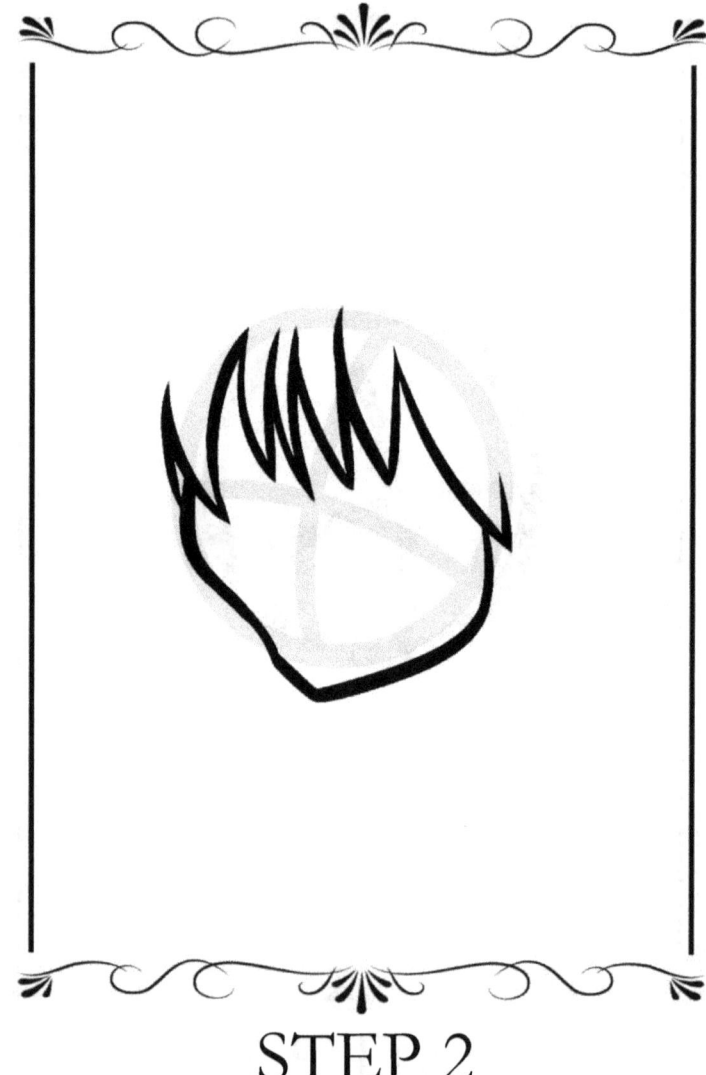

STEP 2

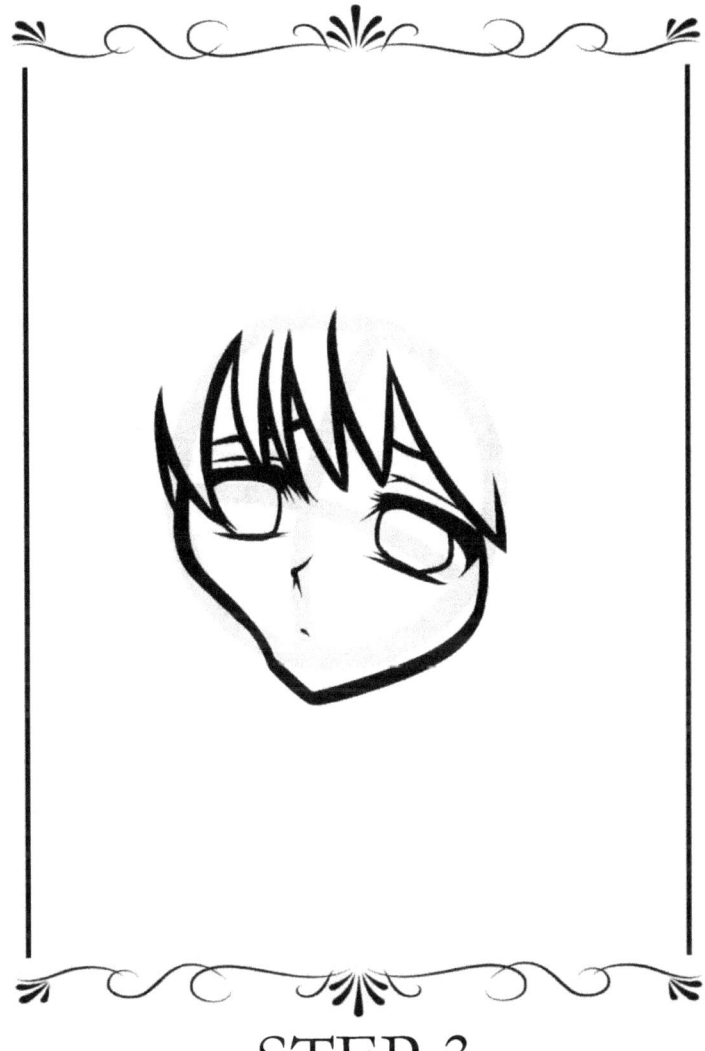

STEP 3

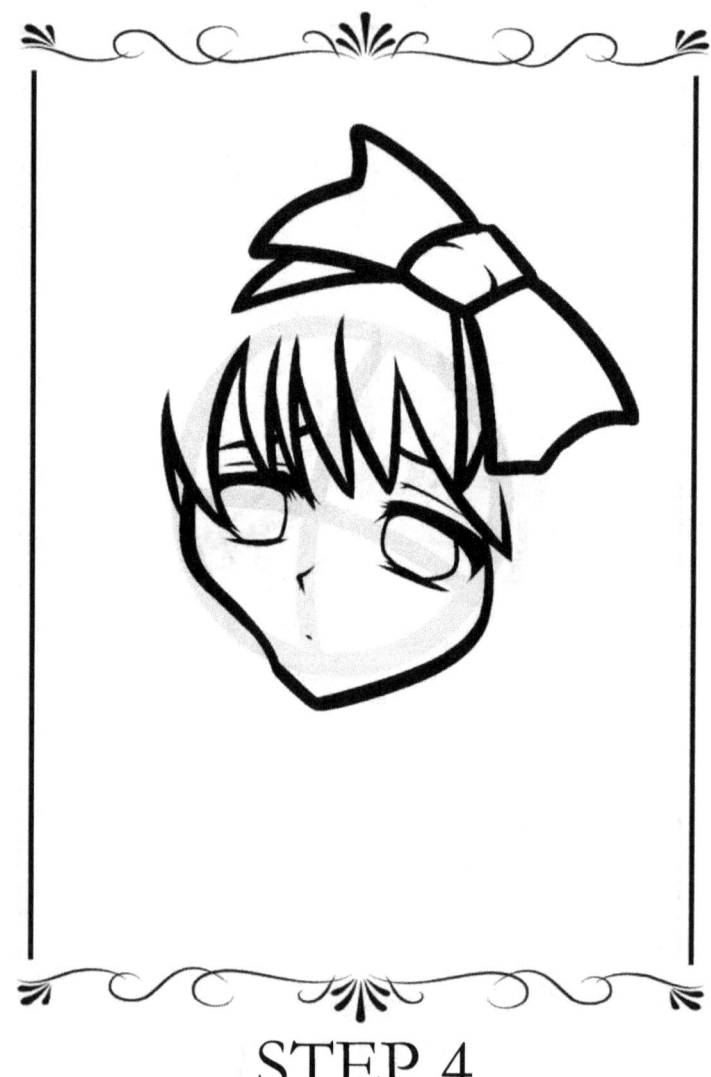

STEP 4

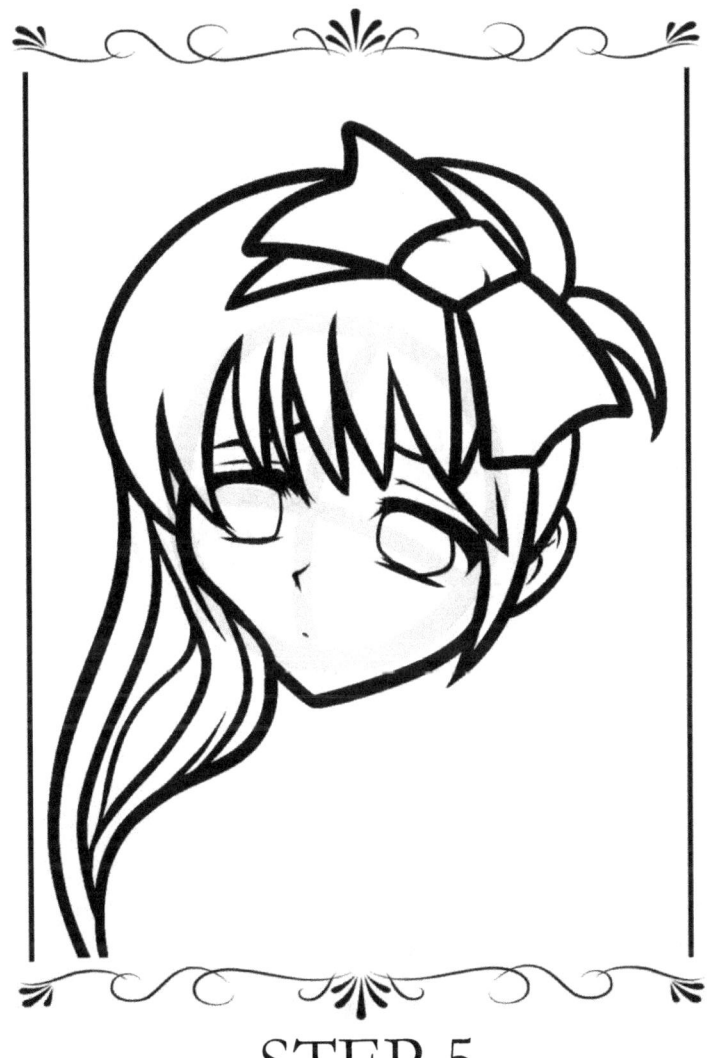

STEP 5

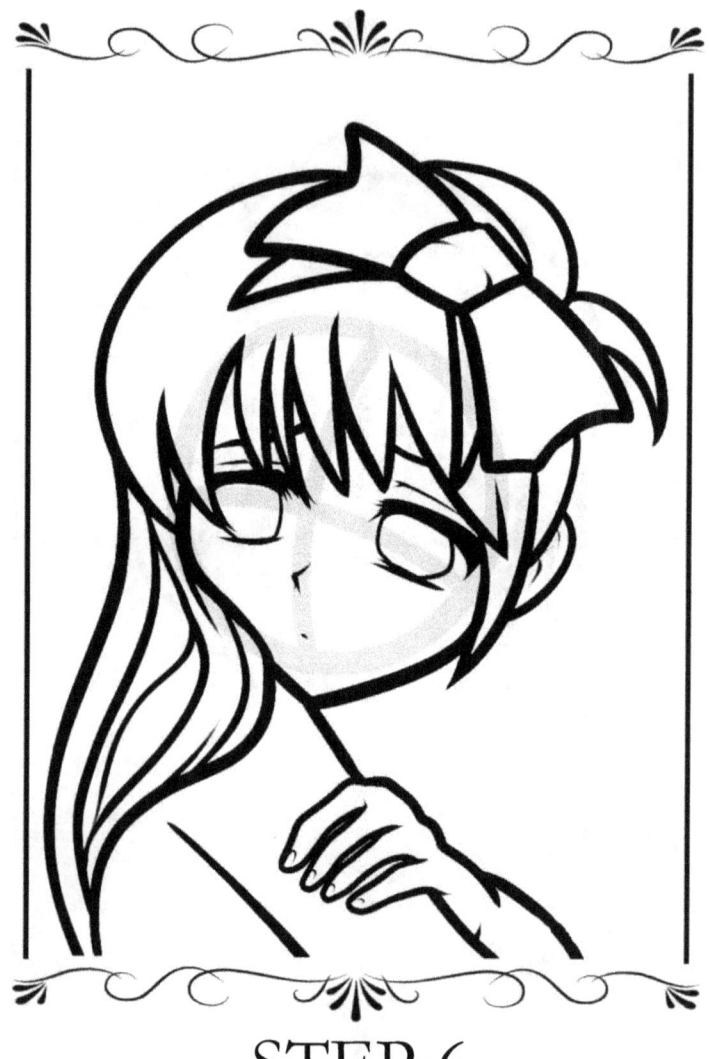

STEP 6

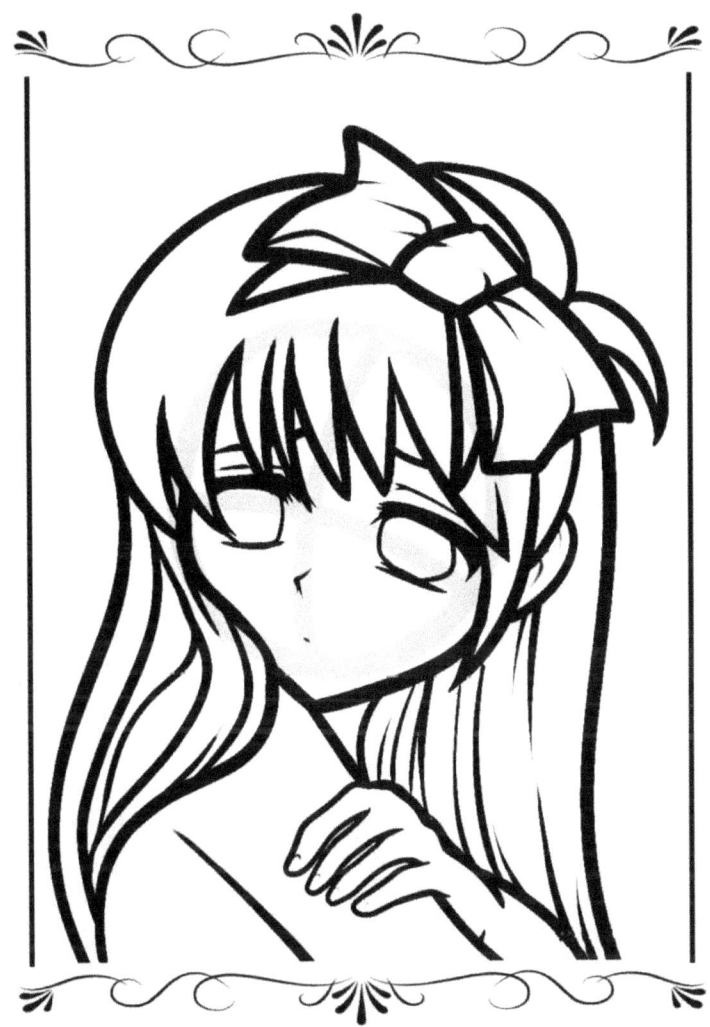

STEP 7

www.ingramcontent.com/pod-product-compliance
Lightning Source LLC
Chambersburg PA
CBHW071543170526
45166CB00004B/1526